Tom Carter is a barrister at Ropewalk Chambers. He has been consistently ranked as a leading barrister for property law, with the 2021 edition of the Legal 500 recognising that he is: "a particularly notable figure within the team for his specialism in cases relating to Japanese knotweed, having recently appeared in several agenda-setting nuisance, misrepresentation and professional negligence cases around infestations of the invasive species".

Tom acted as sole counsel for the successful claimant, Mr Williams, in the case of Network Rail v Williams [2018] EWCA Civ 1514, the leading case on liability in nuisance for Japanese knotweed. He is currently instructed by claimants and defendants in well over 100 ongoing knotweed cases, many of which are likely to set the agenda on a number of important issues.

A Practical Guide to the Law in Relation to Japanese Knotweed and Other Invasive Plants

A Practical Guide to the Law in Relation to Japanese Knotweed and Other Invasive Plants

Tom Carter
Barrister, Inner Temple

Law Brief Publishing

Published 2021 by Law Brief Publishing, an imprint of Law Brief Publishing Ltd
30 The Parks
Minehead
Somerset
TA24 8BT

www.lawbriefpublishing.com

Paperback: 978-1-913715-55-7

To Siobhan

PREFACE

Japanese knotweed is an invasive plant, introduced to the UK in the mid-nineteenth century. It was introduced as an ornamental plant but now is estimated to affect over 2% of development sites and 1.25% of residential properties, according to a House of Commons report in 2019.

Even if your home is not affected by Japanese knotweed, there is no escape from it: if you sell your home, you will have to declare whether or not the property is affected by it when completing the Law Society's property information form.

An entire industry has developed around treating Japanese knotweed: on any motorway, it will not be long before you see a van emblazoned with the logo of one of the many companies including the words "Japanese knotweed" in their name. No doubt the van will be on its way to carry out treatment at yet another affected property.

At the time of writing this book, there is only one binding authority on Japanese knotweed, in the form of the Court of Appeal's decision in *Network Rail Infrastructure Ltd v Williams* [2018] EWCA Civ 1514. This was a landmark case establishing that the mere presence of Japanese knotweed within a claimant's boundaries is enough to constitute a nuisance without the need for physical damage.

There have been other cases at trial generating other widespread interest and media attention but to date, Williams is the only case that has been litigated on appeal.

No doubt in future years, there will a wider range of authorities giving definitive answers to some of the difficult questions that arise in knotweed cases. I am involved in a few claims currently approaching trial likely to give rise to further guidance on a variety of difficult issues, including causation and limitation.

The world is also not standing still outside the confines of litigation. It is thought that the so-called "seven-metre rule" for Japanese knotweed may be exaggerated. There are questions over the extent of damage which Japanese knotweed can cause to properties. There is due to be updated guidance from the Royal Institute of Chartered Surveyors though this is already overdue and there is no date for publication in sight.

In this new and uncertain landscape, the courts have to approach knot-weed claims by drawing principles from other areas and considering how those apply.

The aim of this book is to give a concise but comprehensive summary of those principles and how they will apply. This should give you a steady footing for any claim, be it in nuisance, professional negligence or misrepresentation, whether you act for a claimant or a defendant.

The law quoted in this book is believed to be accurate as at 15 March 2021.

Tom Carter
March 2021

CONTENTS

PART ONE

NUISANCE CLAIMS

CHAPTER ONE

THE ELEMENTS OF A NUISANCE CLAIM

To establish a claim in nuisance, a claimant must show that the defendant owed them a duty of care, was in breach of that duty and the breach of duty caused the claimant loss.

Before getting onto those points, however, the claimant must show that there is something which is capable of being an actionable nuisance in the first place. The aim of this chapter is to consider what needs to be satisfied for a claimant to show a nuisance from the presence of Japanese knotweed.

To establish a nuisance, a claimant must show that:

There is Japanese knotweed within the boundaries of their land;

It has encroached onto their land from the defendant's land.

Unlike claims for encroachment of tree roots, there is no need to show physical damage in order to establish a nuisance in relation to Japanese knotweed.

This was established in the leading case on liability for Japanese knotweed in the Court of Appeal's decision in *Network Rail v Williams* [2018] EWCA Civ 1514.

This was a claim by two neighbours, both of whom owned houses that backed onto a railway line owned by Network Rail. There was Japanese knotweed growing on the railway embankment adjacent to their houses. At trial, the Recorder held that knotweed had encroached from Network

Rail's land onto the claimants' land but that there was no physical damage.

The Recorder considered the three types of nuisance set out by Lord Lloyd in *Hunter v Canary Wharf* [1997] AC 655 at 695C:

i. Nuisance by encroachment on a neighbour's land;

ii. Nuisance by direct physical injury to a neighbour's land;

iii. Nuisance by interference with a neighbour's quiet enjoyment of their land.

He held that on the authorities, a type 1 nuisance nevertheless required physical damage. On that basis, he held that there was no actionable type 1 nuisance.

A type 2 nuisance was never in issue because there was no evidence of physical damage.

The Recorder did find an actionable type 3 nuisance. He held that the presence of Japanese knotweed on the defendant's land, close to the boundary with the claimants' land, was sufficient to interfere with their quiet enjoyment of their land because it may nevertheless affect the sale price and this was an interference with their quiet enjoyment of the land.

In the Court of Appeal, the Master of the Rolls warned against a rigid categorisation of nuisance claims in this way (para 41) but to explain the decision, I will use the type 1 and type 3 analysis above. The Court of Appeal took the opposite approach to the Recorder and held that there was a type 1 nuisance but not a type 3 nuisance.

The Court of Appeal held that unlike tree roots, Japanese knotweed is in itself a hazard and that it will diminish the amenity value of land even without physical damage. On that basis, a claimant need only show the presence of knotweed on their land. At para 55 it was said:

> *"Its presence, and indeed the mere presence of its rhizomes, imposes an immediate burden on the owner of the land in terms of an increased difficulty in the ability to develop, and in the cost of developing, the land, should the owner wish to do so. As the RICS paper observed, any improvement or alteration of the property requiring the removal of contaminated soil would require disposal of the soil either on site or, more likely, off site by special, and probably expensive, procedures. For all those reasons, Japanese knotweed and its rhizomes can fairly be described, in the sense of the decided cases, as a "natural hazard". They affect the owner's ability fully to use and enjoy the land. They are a classic example of an interference with the amenity value of the land."*

And at para 73:

> *"In short, there is no reason why the legal position concerning nuisance caused by the encroachment of the branches or roots of trees should undermine the right of the claimants in the present case to claim damages for nuisance by reason of the encroachment of Japanese knotweed and its rhizomes from NR's land."*

It should be noted in respect of the increased difficulty in developing land referred to in para 55 that there was no evidence from either of the claimants about plans to develop the land. It is the difficulty in principle that constitutes the interference.

The Court of Appeal did, however, reject the Recorder's finding that presence of knotweed on the defendant's land close to the boundary was enough to establish a type 3 nuisance per para 46:

> *"The Recorder's conclusion that the presence of knotweed on NR's land within seven metres of the claimants' properties was an actionable nuisance simply because it diminished the market value of the claimants' respective properties, because of lender caution in such situations, was wrong in principle."*

This paragraph has caused confusion amongst some lawyers who have taken it as authority that a claimant cannot recover damages for diminution in value at all. This is wrong and I set out why in more detail in chapter 6 on diminution in value but for present purposes, the paragraph is clear authority that there cannot be liability in nuisance for knotweed outside of a claimant's boundaries.

One exception to this, outside the scope of a nuisance claim, might be a claim under Article 1 Protocol 1 of the ECHR. I consider this in chapter 10.

CHAPTER TWO

ENCROACHMENT

Once a claimant establishes that there is Japanese knotweed within the boundaries of their land, it is then necessary to show that it encroached onto that land from the defendant's land. If not, the presence of Japanese knotweed may be a nuisance but it was not caused by the Defendant. On that basis, the claim fails for causation.

In some cases, encroachment may be easy to prove. For instance, if there is a large stand of mature knotweed on the defendant's lane and a small amount of knotweed on the claimant's land then this would suggest that it must have spread from the larger growth on the defendant's land.

This is not always the case and it can be dangerous to make assumptions. There may be other reasons for differences in size or maturity of knotweed such as different subsoil, the presence of hard-standings obstructing growth or the effects of herbicide treatment.

The question of encroachment will nearly always turn on expert evidence from a Japanese knotweed expert. There is no technical name for these experts: they may be horticulturalists but they are not normally referred to as such in the context of knotweed claims, unlike arboriculturists in tree root claims. They are simply referred to as "Japanese knotweed experts".

Any reputable knotweed expert will be registered with the Property Care Association (PCA).

There are often initial reports which may be written with one eye on potential litigation but which are not usually CPR part 35 compliant. Claimants will often contact a treatment company before contacting solicitors so the initial report may well be the earliest detailed record of the state of the knotweed. There will usually be a plan showing the locations of knotweed and photographs. For that reason, the reports are often referred back to at trial as lay evidence but they may not go into detailed considerations of encroachment.

Ultimately the question is a simple one in most cases: is it more likely than not that the Japanese knotweed on the claimant's land originated from the defendant's land?

There may be Japanese knotweed on more than one adjacent property. This may complicate a claim if the ages and sizes of the various stands of Japanese knotweed are similar. Generally, this will be something that the Japanese knotweed expert needs to consider.

Sometimes, knotweed on adjacent properties may be a red herring if the knotweed is not right up to the boundary. For instance, if two adjacent properties back onto a strip of land with Japanese knotweed but the knotweed on each property is spread quite far apart, this might suggest that they are simply two separate stands of knotweed.

Sometimes, it may be established that Japanese knotweed has encroached onto a claimant's land from multiple properties. If so, this may raise a question about concurrent causes which I consider in the context of causation in chapter 5.

An important question may also be *when* Japanese knotweed encroached. Not only is this often crucial in misrepresentation claims but it may be relevant in nuisance claims as well.

If Japanese knotweed encroached before a defendant came under a duty to treat it, defendants will generally argue that the claim fails the but for test.

Imagine that knotweed encroached in 2010 and the court finds that the defendant came under a duty to treat the knotweed in 2012. The court also finds that the defendant did not treat and so was in breach of duty from 2012 onwards. Had the defendant complied with its duty, the knotweed had already encroached and so the breach made no difference.

How does this affect the claim?

There is no decided authority on this point but my own view is that the issue may be relevant to treatment costs but not to other losses.

The reason for this is that even if knotweed would always have encroached, it is futile for a claimant to treat the knotweed on their land until the defendant is reasonably treating its own land. Otherwise, knotweed will re-encroach onto the claimant's land and defeat the point of treatment.

In the example above, the claimant might say that had the defendant started treating when it came under a duty, the claimant could then have started treatment (albeit having to pay the costs) and the knotweed would or should have been eradicated, or at least closer to being eradicated. If so, the defendant's breach of duty from 2012 onwards has caused a delay in the eradication of the knotweed.

If that analysis is correct, a claimant would still have a claim for diminution in value against the defendant on the basis that its delay has allowed the diminution to continue for longer than it should have done. I discuss diminution in value in chapter 6 but in summary, most expert surveyors will say that it is based on both mortgage lender caution and purchaser stigma. Certainly for purchaser stigma, a homeowner would need to declare in question 7.8 of the Law Society's property information form that the property is affected by Japanese knotweed if an insurance-backed guarantee remains in place. That will alert any potential purchaser and the stigma remains. If that period runs for 10 years then a delay on the part of the defendant means that the clock did not start ticking as early as it should have done, extending the period of diminution. There is an argument about whether a reduction to any award of damages for diminution should be reduced in that context.

All of this only arises in cases where encroachment occurred before the defendant was under a duty. It is for that reason that the date of encroachment will often be important.

CHAPTER THREE

DUTY OF CARE

Once it is shown that there is Japanese knotweed within the boundaries of a claimant's land and that it is more likely than not that it has spread from the defendant's land, in what circumstances does the defendant owe a duty of care?

The starting point is that it is immaterial whether or not the defendant planted the knotweed or actively caused it to grow or spread. It is well-established that a defendant may be liable for a nuisance if they adopt or continue it: *Sedleigh Denfield v O'Callaghan* [1940] AC 880 (HL). In this context, to continue a nuisance means to fail to take reasonable steps to prevent it i.e. non-feasance. This rule extends to liability for naturals hazards and not only man-made ones: *Leakey v National Trust* [1980] QB 485 (CA).

Therefore, the question is when the defendant did or should have known both of the following: firstly, knowledge that Japanese knotweed is an invasive plant and secondly, that Japanese knotweed was present on the defendant's land.

Depending on the type of defendant, the first or second of these may be the key issue. For instance, a local authority with thousands of acres of land may have known for some time that Japanese knotweed is an invasive plant but may argue that it did not know that there was Japanese knotweed in an area of one of its parks.

Conversely, a residential homeowner with a small garden would be bound to know that Japanese knotweed was present if it was there to be seen from the kitchen window but might argue that they did not know that it was an invasive plant.

In terms of knowledge, this can be actual knowledge or constructive knowledge. Within the ambit of constructive knowledge, there is also the question of specialist knowledge.

Actual knowledge is straightforward: it is when the defendant actually knew of the knotweed. The key evidence is usually a record of any complaints from the claimant or someone nearby. Sometimes, a local resident will complain about Japanese knotweed to the council and an environmental officer will visit or send a letter to the defendant. Sometimes, actual knowledge might be inferred from the fact that the defendant was seen trying to remove the knotweed by a neighbour.

Arguments on actual knowledge will usually come down to the strength of the evidence. Defendants will often deny having received a complaint unless there is a written record of it. Where there is a letter from the council, it will nearly always be denied that this was received.

Against institutional defendants such as Network Rail, the Environment Agency or local authorities, not only may there be evidence of former complaints about Japanese knotweed from other properties but there will usually be other documents showing treatment records or policies for treating Japanese knotweed. All of this will show actual knowledge about Japanese knotweed being an invasive plant. The battleground will then be knowledge of knotweed in a particular location.

Constructive knowledge is based on what a reasonable person in the defendant's position should have known: the defendant is then fixed with that knowledge.

In *Network Rail Infrastructure Ltd v Williams* [2018] EWCA Civ 1514, there was no challenge in the Court of Appeal to the Recorder's finding at trial that Network Rail had constructive knowledge that Japanese knotweed was an invasive plant and that it was present near to the claimants' homes from 2012/13.

Given that finding was made in the County Court, it is not binding, but my experience has been that all other judges have followed this approach in Japanese knotweed claims.

The reasoning for that approach is that from 2012 onwards, there was a marked shift in terms of awareness of the dangers of Japanese knotweed. Its invasiveness had been known about for some time before this but in 2012, there was guidance published from RICS ("Japanese knotweed and residential property") about the dangers of Japanese knotweed. It was held that following this, a reasonable person in the defendant's position should have known about it.

The reasoning for the 2012/13 rather than simply 2012 was to allow some time thereafter to identify knotweed near to the claimants' properties in the course of carrying out a reasonable system of inspection.

Where the defendant owns large amounts of land, arguments on inspection will often be key. Defendants will argue that it would be an unduly onerous burden to expect regular inspections of large amounts of land and may seek to rely on a purely reactive system based on complaints. Claimants will argue that this a system of proactive inspection is reasonably required given the dangers of Japanese knotweed and that staff should also be trained to identify it while on the defendant's land doing other work.

There is no binding authority on what is required in terms of inspection. The decision in *Williams* suggests that a year was a reasonable period though there may be different factors at play for different defendants.

What then of specialist knowledge? This is a concept flowing from the Supreme Court's decision in the case of *Baker v Quantum Clothing Group Ltd* [2011] UKSC 17. A defendant with subjectively higher knowledge will be held to a higher standard than another defendant without that knowledge.

This approach has been expressly adopted into nuisance cases involving tree roots in *Khan v Harrow Council & Kane* [2013] EWHC 2687 (TCC). There, the subjective approach was described as creating a floor not a ceiling.

The effect of this is that all defendants are held to the same objective standard, and no defendant can rely on its own subjective ignorance to lower that standard, but a defendant who does have specialist knowledge on a subject will be held to that higher standard.

In the context of a Japanese knotweed claim, this may mean that a professional gardener would be held to a higher standard when considering constructive knowledge than a layperson.

For large institutional defendants, disclosure of policies, documents and records relating to Japanese knotweed will be important because it may transpire that a particular defendant did have specialist knowledge.

There is some overlap with actual knowledge. For instance, a defendant may be found to have known about the invasiveness of Japanese knotweed from at least the 2000s. On that point, the defendant had actual knowledge of this fact. The claimant would then argue that based on this, the defendant should have implemented a system of inspection in the 2000s and therefore had constructive knowledge of Japanese knotweed near to the claimant's property within one year of that date because it would or should have been discovered on a reasonable inspection.

CHAPTER FOUR

BREACH OF DUTY

Once a defendant has knowledge of Japanese knotweed, in principle and in a particular location, it comes under a duty to do something about it. What is required of a defendant in order to comply with its duty?

As in any case, the standard required in order to comply with the duty is not one of perfection. It is an objective question of reasonableness, having regard to all the circumstances of the case. This principle can be found in a multitude of authorities in all areas of the common law but in this context, the case of *Vernon Knight Associates v Cornwall Council* [2013] EWCA Civ 950 is relevant.

The three key points from that decision are as follows:

i. The defendant owes a "measured duty" to take reasonable care to prevent damage to a neighbouring claimant from natural hazards on its land.

ii. The court will consider what is fair, just and reasonable, taking into account the extent of foreseeable risk, the availability of preventative measures and their cost and the resources of both parties.

iii. Where the defendant is a public authority with substantial resources, the court will consider the competing demands on those resources.

The duty is often referred to as a duty to treat. This is convenient shorthand because that will normally be the minimum standard expected of any defendant. Despite the problems caused by Japanese knotweed, the process to get rid of it is fairly straightforward (albeit it still takes a long period of time).

The knotweed can be treated with herbicide or it can be excavated. I discuss damages for treatment costs in chapter 7 but herbicide treatment is generally cheaper because it does not involve excavating potentially huge quantities of soil. There are plenty of reputable treatment companies who will implement a four to five-year herbicide treatment plan with insurance-backed guarantee for a modest sum, usually between £3,000 to £5,000.

Given this, even if the defendant is an individual with limited means, or argues that as a public authority it has other competing demands on its resources, it is difficult to see how it would escape a finding that it was required to implement a system of herbicide treatment in order to comply with its duty. Certainly, that was the finding of the Recorder at trial in *Network Rail Infrastructure Ltd v Williams* [2018] EWCA Civ 1514, not then challenged on appeal.

Depending on the defendant, it may use its own staff to treat the knotweed or may engage a third-party contractor. The benefit to the defendant of using its own staff may be cost but those advising a defendant should be aware of the risks involved in this approach. I have seen many cases, acting for both claimants and defendants, of employees purporting to carry out herbicide treatment which has not been done properly.

For instance, the knotweed must be sprayed methodically and consistently. Japanese knotweed experts will often be able to identify signs of herbicide treatment from "bonsai growth", which is generally weakened growth with signs of stem twisting. This is characteristic of the rhizomes from which those stems have grown being treated with herbicide.

Where the stand of knotweed is large, it is often the case that parts will be missed. If so, some stems will show signs of herbicide treatment but others will not. The knotweed which has not been treated will then continue to grow unabated.

Arguments on the quality of herbicide treatment do not go to a resources argument. Once a defendant begins to treat, it costs no more to do this properly than to do it badly.

There are other factors which may undermine the effectiveness of herbicide treatment: for example, spraying on a very windy day or attending the site shortly after herbicide treatment and cutting down the stems before the herbicide has had time to translocate to the rhizomes.

Where treatment has taken place, it will be important for a defendant to keep a proper record of treatment. At a minimum, this should normally involve recording the weather conditions, the herbicide used and the dosage rate together with the metres squared of knotweed which has been sprayed. If a defendant does not keep these records, it may run into difficulties later in proving that treatment has been reasonable.

It will also be important to have a treatment plan in place and for herbicide to be sprayed consistently. Normally, a treatment plan will involve the application of herbicide once or twice per year. If a defendant begins treatment but then misses a year, that missed year may well amount to a breach of duty.

If a defendant uses its own employees to treat the knotweed, it will also be important to be able to evidence the training and qualifications of those staff.

In order to consider the reasonableness of treatment, it will normally be required for parties to rely on expert evidence from a Japanese knotweed expert. This will usually be the same expert who has commented on encroachment as discussed in chapter 2.

There are certain circumstances where it may be inferred that treatment has not been done reasonably. For instance, if a defendant has purported to treat a stand of knotweed for over five years but there is little, if any, sign of the stand reducing in size, the court may infer that it has not been done properly.

Effective herbicide treatment will reduce the size of a stand of knotweed on a proportional basis meaning that the same rate of reduction should be expected in a large stand as in a small stand. While there is no hard and fast rule, certainly it would normally be expected that the knotweed has been eradicated or almost eradicated after four or five years.

The court will inevitably allow some leeway but if there has been little significant reduction in the knotweed after five years, this does tend to suggest that it has not been treated properly.

CHAPTER FIVE

CAUSATION

Any nuisance claim must follow the basic proposition that in order to recover damages, a claimant must prove that those damages have been caused by the defendant's breach of duty.

In *Network Rail Infrastructure Ltd v Williams* [2018] EWCA Civ, the Court of Appeal considered causation as a ground of appeal but the defendant had not adduced evidence on this from its expert at trial. On that basis, there is very limited guidance on causation to be found in that case and there are no other reported authorities on point.

There are all sorts of potential arguments on causation. For example, what if Japanese knotweed on the claimant's land is found to have spread from two neighbouring properties, each owned by a separate defendant? What if only one of those defendants is found to have been in breach of duty: would the defendant in breach be liable for the whole loss, a portion of the loss or none of the loss?

The courts have grappled with similar issues in other areas. One relevant question may be whether losses caused by Japanese knotweed are divisible or indivisible. Divisible losses are dose-related (for example, damage to hearing caused by noise). The need for treatment and diminution in value will tend to arise as long as there is *any* knotweed present at a property. On that basis, it would seem to be an indivisible loss.

There is authority, in the context of defamation, that defendants are liable for the whole of an indivisible loss: *Dingle v Associated Newspapers* [1972] AC 601 (HL). There, the House of Lords held that a claimant's damages following a defamatory newspaper article did not fall to be reduced because his reputation had already been harmed by things said about him in Parliament, where a cause of action was barred by privilege.

While it is a separate cause of action to nuisance, defamation is still founded in tort (albeit now supplemented by statute in the Defamation Act 2013). The authorities are clear that there is no real difference between negligence and nuisance, instead those simply being labels to deal with the question of a reasonable apportionment of responsible conduct between neighbours: *Delaware Mansions v Lord Mayor* [2001] UKHL 55. The court might conclude that in this context, the same approach to causation as in *Dingle* should apply in nuisance.

One issue where causation may be relevant is the date of encroachment of Japanese knotweed. Where knotweed encroached before the defendant came under a duty to treat it, the defendant may argue that its breach of duty made no difference because the loss had already occurred and so the claim fails the but for test. I consider this issue in chapter 2 and my view is that this argument may defeat a claim for treatment costs but not for other damages (including diminution in value) if the claimant can show an unreasonable delay in starting to treat.

CHAPTER SIX

DIMINUTION IN VALUE

A claim for diminution in value is often the most hotly contested issue in a nuisance case. The simple reason for this is that it is usually the largest head of loss, normally by a significant margin.

Before considering the legal concepts, the starting point is that there will always need to be expert valuation evidence from a surveyor to deal with diminution in value. The surveyor's job is ultimately to value the property without Japanese knotweed and then to compare this to its value with Japanese knotweed. The difference is the diminution in value.

Sometimes, an expert surveyor will not have knowledge of the local property market in the area of the claimant's property and so it is often the case that they will be assisted by valuations from local estate agents. The surveyor can normally be asked if they would prefer this before they are formally instructed: if so, valuations from local estate agents can be obtained and then sent to the surveyor with their instructions.

There are two kinds of diminution in value. These tend to be referred to as full diminution in value and residual diminution in value.

Full diminution in value is the difference in price between the property without knotweed and with knotweed that remains untreated.

Residual diminution in value is the difference in price between the property without knotweed and with Japanese knotweed but after a treatment plan with an insurance-backed guarantee is in place.

The figure for full diminution in value will be higher, but in all cases the court is overwhelmingly likely to award the lower figure for the residual diminution in value plus treatment costs.

The reason for this is that damages for full diminution in value would tend to over-compensate a claimant. Take an example of a property worth £200,000. An expert surveyor values it at £150,000 with Japanese knotweed. The full diminution figure is £50,000. With a treatment plan in place costing £4,000, the property would be worth £180,000. The residual diminution is £20,000 and treatment would cost £4,000 (so damages are £24,000 in total).

In those circumstances, were the court to award damages for full diminution of £50,000 then the claimant could spend £4,000 on treatment, have that diminution reduced to £20,000 and then have a windfall of £26,000 (£50,000 minus £24,000).

It is therefore crucial to ensure that the surveyor is instructed to comment on the value of the property without knotweed and the residual diminution in value. They may also comment on the full diminution but that figure is unlikely to be relevant.

There are two main causes of diminution in value. The first is lender caution. It has been the case before that many mortgage lenders simply would not lend a purchaser money to buy a house where Japanese knotweed was present. Often this would be detected during the mortgage valuation report. Sometimes, an owner would only discover the presence of Japanese knotweed when trying to re-mortgage and a surveyor would then identify it. The consequence of lender caution is that if trying to sell their home, a claimant might only be able to sell to cash buyers or at auction, usually for less money.

The issue of lender caution has become less of a problem in recent years because most (or at least many) mortgage lenders will now lend against properties as long as there is a treatment plan with insurance-backed guarantee in place.

The second main cause of diminution in value is purchaser stigma. Often, a buyer might make an offer on a home which is accepted but they later obtain a survey which identifies Japanese knotweed. Alternatively, the seller may declare that the property is affected by Japanese knotweed at question 7.8 of the Law Society's property information form (considered in chapter 11) as they are bound to do if they know that it is present.

If so, the buyer may well pull out or insist on a lower price. Though Japanese knotweed can be treated effectively, the process takes many years and it may later re-emerge. In the meantime, the use of that area of the property will be restricted and if the buyers later wanted to sell the property, they themselves would have to declare that it was affected by Japanese knotweed.

The consequence of this is that for many purchasers, they may simply decide that it is too uncertain and too much hassle, and would rather buy a similar property nearby that does not have knotweed.

In terms of figures, generally one would see a residual diminution in value in the region of 3-5% for a residential property. This will of course depend on the surveyor's evidence in a particular case and there may well be factors to justify a higher or lower percentage than this.

For commercial properties, the same principles of diminution in value apply. The surveyor will need to take the nature of the property into consideration when assessing diminution in value but ultimately the approach is similar.

One potential change on the horizon is updated guidance from the Royal Institute of Chartered Surveyors. The existing guidance dates from 2012 and following a House of Commons report on Japanese knotweed in the built environment, updated guidance has been requested. This guidance was originally due by the end of 2019 and so is already well over one year late. There is no imminent date of publication at the time of writing.

It is thought that the updated guidance will reflect a greater understanding of the dangers of physical damage to property from Japanese knotweed. It remains to be seen what it will say and whether this will change the landscape for claims for diminution in value but I anticipate that it will not.

The principal reason for this is that even if the updated guidance concludes that Japanese knotweed is not as dangerous as previously thought, it will remain an invasive plant needing treatment over a long period of time and many lenders or purchasers will still prefer to steer clear of it.

Even if the guidance concluded that Japanese knotweed were entirely innocuous (which is unlikely), a property owner trying to sell their property would be reliant on the public at large being well-informed about the latest guidance and factoring that into their decision. The reality is that most purchasers will be uninformed and would simply prefer to err on the side of caution and not take the risk. It is no consolation to a property owner who can only sell their property at a reduced value to say that the purchasers refusing to buy it for more are being irrational.

In those circumstances, I would suggest that the question is who should bear the burden of that risk. It seems to me that the only sensible answer to this is that the tortfeasor must bear the risk: that is consistent with the law's approach in other areas.

If correct then the impact of updated RICS guidance at some point in the future is likely to have very little impact.

CHAPTER SEVEN

TREATMENT COSTS

The normal approach for the court to take when assessing damages for nuisance from Japanese knotweed is to look at the residual diminution in value of the property plus the cost of treatment.

I discuss diminution in value in chapter 6: the residual diminution is the diminution in value once a treatment plan and insurance-backed guarantee is in place.

If the court does award damages for the residual diminution, the claimant should be entitled to the costs of treatment because it is only that treatment which enables a claimant to mitigate their loss and to reduce the diminution in value from the full figure to the residual figure.

Firstly, should treatment costs be for herbicide treatment or for excavation?

Herbicide treatment is usually the cheaper option and involves a four to five-year treatment plan where Japanese knotweed will be sprayed with a herbicide (usually glyphosate) once or twice per year until eradicated. The herbicide can either be applied with a sprayer or injected into the knotweed stems. This is done during the growing season and the herbicide translocates into the rhizomes, killing the plant.

The knotweed is considered to be eradicated when there is no more visual growth during a growing season. There will likely still be rhizomes in the soil which may remain dormant for up to 20 years so it is not truly eradicated. At this point, there should be a 10-year insurance-backed guarantee that then begins. This is a guarantee that if knotweed re-emerges within that 10-year period from eradication, the treatment provider will re-attend and start a new course of treatment.

The insurance-backed guarantee provides reassurance to the property owner that if the treatment provider ceases trading during that time, the policy will fund the cost of another treatment provider.

Excavation involves removing all soil potentially contaminated by Japanese knotweed rhizomes. There are various methods of doing this employed by different treatment companies but the most straightforward is often referred to as "dig and dump". It involves, as the name suggests, simply digging out the soil and disposing of it.

Excavation is usually more expensive, not least because it will tend to involve excavating very large amounts of soil. Rhizomes can be present quite deep into the ground and are known to have a large lateral spread. The seven-metre rule is now thought to be overstated but rhizomes can certainly spread at least two to three metres in any direction from visible knotweed stems.

Excavation should also be followed with an insurance-backed guarantee to cover the possibility that some knotweed has been missed.

Claimants will often prefer excavation because it is a quicker solution that herbicide treatment. Inevitably, defendants will be unlikely to want to pay the additional costs of excavation when herbicide treatment, if done properly, is known to be effective.

There are also downsides to excavation in certain circumstances: for instance, if rhizomes are present in concrete foundations, they cannot be excavated without undermining the structure. Herbicide treatment can, however, be applied to knotweed stems growing from those rhizomes and it will then translocate into the rhizomes beneath the structure.

There is an argument that while the costs of excavation are greater, it may reduce the residual diminution in value of the property. I discuss this in the context of diminution in chapter 6 but in conclusion, I think it is unlikely that this is really the case. Given the cheaper cost of herbicide treatment, this is another indicator that in most cases, the court will tend towards herbicide costs rather than excavation.

There are some exceptions to this. For instance, the claimant may be a building developer with a limited period of time to finish building homes before planning permission expires. In certain circumstances, the additional costs of excavation may be justified.

In either case, there will need to be a quote for treatment costs. Often, an early quote is obtained by the claimant pre-litigation. The parties will generally be wise to obtain up-to-date quotes at the time of any updated schedule of loss and counter-schedule.

CHAPTER EIGHT

REPAIRS AND OTHER LOSSES

While it is now thought that the danger of physical damage to houses from Japanese knotweed was previously overstated, it does remain the case that it can and will cause damage to all sorts of property, including patios, garden fences and sheds.

Where there is damage, a claimant can recover for this but the crucial issue is often whether they can show that the damage was caused by the knotweed.

In certain cases, this may be straightforward. For example, damage to a patio where there are Japanese knotweed rhizomes underneath can usually be taken to have been caused by the knotweed.

In other cases, it may be difficult to establish whether damage was caused by knotweed or whether it is simply deterioration through age. For instance, a wooden boundary fence may have been in situ for decades. There may be visible damage on the part of the boundary where Japanese knotweed has encroached, suggesting that damage has been caused by the knotweed, but the fence is unlikely to be in perfect condition in other areas.

In cases where property damage from knotweed is alleged, a claimant will nearly always need expert evidence on causation. It will usually be the expert surveyor who is asked to comment on this alongside reporting on diminution in value. A defendant can likewise ask its surveyor to comment on this when providing their report.

Sometimes, certain items of garden furniture will have to be removed in order to treat Japanese knotweed at the property. For example, it is often the case that a claimant will be asked to remove a garden shed. If so, the claimant may be able to recover damages for this. Causation is usually more straightforward in this case because its removal clearly flows from the presence of Japanese knotweed. If its removal is recommended by a reputable treatment provider, it would be difficult to criticise a claimant for following this advice.

For all of these claims, the basic principle will apply that damages are valued on a like-for-like basis. In the example of a garden shed, damages would be for the value of the shed in its present condition and age, which may well be significantly less than the value of a new shed.

There are various ways in which the parties can approach this. Given the sums in dispute will generally be modest, the court may well accept an approach of looking at an invoice for the original item if available, or a quote for a new equivalent and then applying a percentage discount to account for age and pre-existing damage. If so, the percentage would normally be based on the expected lifespan of the item. A shed might be expected to last 20 years: if so, a 10-year old shed which has to be removed to allow treatment of knotweed would logically be worth 50% of a new equivalent.

Limitation will often be critical in claims for repairs and other losses. I discuss limitation for all types of claims in chapter 20, and for nuisance claims in general there is the principle of a continuing nuisance. This does still provide, however, that damages incurred more than six years before the claim is brought will not be recoverable.

Claims for physical damage to fences, patios and sheds etc. will operate in the same way as physical damage in the case of subsidence from tree roots, where it is well-established that damage shown to have occurred more than six years before the claim is brought will not be recoverable.

On that basis, as well as establishing causation of damage, it will also be important to establish when damage was caused.

A claimant may also have a claim for general damages for distress and inconvenience. This is in line with similar damages in claims for subsidence from tree roots. In those cases, such damages have been described as "modest".

In *Network Rail Infrastructure Ltd v Williams* [2018] EWCA Civ 1514, the Recorder awarded £350 per year at trial, which was not then challenged on appeal.

In that case, there were two claimants, each the sole owner of their respective properties. Where there are co-owners, they may both be entitled to an award of general damages.

The yearly figure will depend on the extent of the Japanese knotweed and how disruptive it is. For instance, knotweed growing right up against the windows of a house will be more disruptive than a small stand of knotweed at the far end of the garden.

Ordinarily, a claimant could expect to recover an award of general damages for each year from breach of duty either to the end of the breach (if the defendant has started complying with its duty before trial) or else to date of trial.

If an owner does not live at the property, they will not be able to recover general damages during that period.

CHAPTER NINE

MITIGATION AND CONTRIBUTORY NEGLIGENCE

A common argument in nuisance claims is that the claimant has themselves been negligent or failed to mitigate their loss. This can be either by not or by not reporting it sooner, failing to treat Japanese knotweed on their own land or potentially making the situation worse by purporting to treat it but doing so poorly.

As far as a claimant reporting Japanese knotweed is concerned, any evidence of reporting is relevant to the date of the defendant's actual knowledge as discussed in chapter 3 but often this will come after the date of constructive knowledge in any event.

If so then it would be surprising for the court to make any reduction in damages to reflect contributory negligence or a failure to mitigate. The reason for this is that the defendant is already fixed with knowledge that it should reasonably have acquired. In those circumstances, it cannot rely on a claimant's failure to report because that failure made no difference: the defendant is already taken as having that knowledge in any event.

There may be circumstances, however, where a failure to report is relevant. For instance, it may be relevant where the defendant is an individual with no particular knowledge of Japanese knotweed. If a claimant were to identify Japanese knotweed on the neighbouring defendant's land but not mention it, it would be open to the court to make a finding of contributory negligence against them if the knotweed later spread.

In respect of a claimant not treating knotweed on their own land once they know it is present, this is a logical argument but my own view is that it will rarely succeed. The reason for this is that unless and until the defendant puts in place a reasonable treatment plan for its own land, it is futile for the claimant to treat knotweed on their land because even if it is eradicated, knotweed is likely to re-encroach from the defendant's land in the future.

One way around this might be to install a root barrier along the boundary but in my experience, Japanese knotweed experts will say that root barriers are not completely effective and also, the cost of installing a root barrier will often be greater than the cost of a treatment plan.

For these reasons, a failure to mitigate argument based on the claimant not treating knotweed on their land will not usually succeed.

There is then the argument where a claimant has actively tried to treat or remove the knotweed but has not done so in a proper way. Sometimes, laypeople will do all sorts of unwise things to try to remove knotweed. Often this will involve pulling shoots out of the ground or cutting it down. Both of these are unhelpful because they prevent the knotweed from being properly treated. The knotweed stems need to remain intact so that when herbicide is sprayed or injected, it can translocate down into the rhizomes and kill the plant. If the stems are removed or cut back, there is nowhere for the herbicide to travel.

Occasionally, a claimant will do something truly novel such as pouring petrol on the Japanese knotweed. I have seen one case where this occurred on a large stand of knotweed covering almost their entire back garden. Thankfully they thought it would kill the knotweed without then setting it on fire. Were their house to be destroyed in the ensuing explosion, you would probably not need this book to tell you that there might be a claim for contributory negligence were they to then allege diminution in value.

There may be other cases where specific arguments on mitigation or contributory negligence arise. An obvious example of contributory negligence may be someone who knows there is knotweed in their back garden but then has building work done and allows the rhizomes to spread, making their situation worse.

PART TWO

ARTICLE 1 PROTOCOL 1

CHAPTER TEN

ARTICLE 1 PROTOCOL 1 CLAIMS

There are contexts where a claimant cannot rely on the tort of nuisance or some other tort to establish liability against a defendant.

For instance, where knotweed is close to his property but he cannot show encroachment. On the authority of *Network Rail v Williams* [2018] EWCA Civ 1514, there cannot be a nuisance in those circumstances. There might still be liability, however, under Article 1 Protocol 1 of the ECHR ("A1P1").

Alternatively, imagine a scenario where a building developer purchases land and applies for planning permission to build a number of houses. During the planning process, local residents complain that the land is affected by Japanese knotweed. The council grants planning permission but with a condition that he treats the knotweed before commencing work. The council then delays in signing off the treatment and he cannot start the work. Either the planning permission lapses or he simply loses money while the land sits unused.

It would be difficult for a claimant to establish a cause of action against the council in those circumstances. He would struggle to establish any kind of assumption of responsibility that could give rise to a duty for pure economic loss.

In those circumstances, he might, however, have a remedy under A1P1.

Whereas a nuisance consists of an interference with the quiet use and enjoyment of land, A1P1 contains the concept of "peaceful enjoyment". The Article provides:

> *"(1) Every natural or legal person is entitled to the peaceful enjoyment of his possessions. No one shall be deprived of his possession except in the public interest and subject to the conditions provided for by law and the general principles of international law.*
>
> *(2) The preceding provisions shall not, however, in any way impair the right of a state to enforce such laws as it deems necessary to control the use of property in accordance with the general interest or to secure the payment of taxes or other contributions or penalties."*

In *Williams*, it was held that diminution in value arising from knotweed on the defendant's land, close to a claimant's land, will not amount to a nuisance. The knotweed must actually have encroached onto the claimant's land, at which point diminution in value may be a consequential loss. The reasoning for this is at para 48:

> *"The purpose of the tort of nuisance is not to protect the value of property as an investment or a financial asset."*

An A1P1 claim, by contrast, does include an economic element. The authorities relating to what amounts as a possession include shares, patents, ownership of a debt and the right to enforce a court order or decision on arbitration. These are all clearly economic interests.

In *Thomas & ors v Bridgend County Borough Council* [2011] EWCA Civ 862, the claimants sought damages for diminution in value of their homes due to noise and nuisance from a new relief road.

In that case, it was explicitly said at para 38:

> *"To summarise, loss of a quiet and pleasant environment, without evidence of loss of value, is not enough to engage Article 1"*

There are two readings of this approach:

i. A claimant needs to show loss of a quiet and pleasant enjoyment and a loss of value;

ii. The only relevant question is loss of value and loss of a quiet and pleasant enjoyment is irrelevant.

The remainder of the decision and the commentary referred to therein tends to suggest that the second reading is correct. That is to say, the scope of A1P1 is only concerned with economic value and a claimant need not prove both.

This suggests that a claimant who cannot show encroachment but who is affected by knotweed on a defendant's land nearby might nevertheless succeed in an A1P1 claim.

The limitation on a claim under Art 1 Protocol 1 is that it is only available against public authorities.

ECHR rights do not have direct effect but are enforceable by virtue of their inclusion in Schedule 1 to the Human Rights Act 1998. Section 6(1) of that Act provides that it is unlawful for a public authority to act in a way which is incompatible with a Convention right.

Under section 6(3) of the Act, a public authority includes "any person certain of whose functions are functions of a public nature" but under section 6(5), not if the act in question is private.

In *Cameron v Network Rail Infrastructure Ltd* [2006] EWHC 1133 (QB), it was held that Network Rail was not acting as a public authority as infrastructure controller of the national railway network at the time of the Potters Bar train crash.

Given this restrictive approach, it seems likely that an A1P1 knotweed claim against Network Rail would fail on the basis that Network Rail was not acting as a public authority.

A public authority will, of course, include councils, as can be seen from the *Thomas* case.

PART THREE

MISREPRESENTATION CLAIMS

CHAPTER ELEVEN

THE TA6 FORM

In most misrepresentation claims, the representation will come from the Law Society's property information form aka "the TA6 form".

On 8 June 2020, the Law Society published the new fourth edition of the TA6 form. For sellers completing the form after this date, they will likely have used the new form. Before this date, sellers likely used the third edition.

For both versions, the relevant section is found at question 7.8.

Both versions ask whether the property is affected by Japanese knotweed. In both, the seller can tick "Yes", "No" or "Not known".

If the seller does tick "Yes", there is a further question in both versions asking for details of any treatment plan.

The difference between the two versions is the preamble.

In the third edition, this reads:

> ***"Japanese knotweed***
>
> ***Note:*** *Japanese knotweed is an invasive plant that can cause damage to property. It can take several years to eradicate."*

The fourth addition has a more detailed preamble which reads:

> ***"Japanese knotweed***
>
> ***Note:** Japanese knotweed is an invasive non-native plant that can cause damage to property if left untreated. The plant consists of visible above ground growth and an invisible rhizome (root) below ground in the soil. It can take several years to control and manage through a management and treatment plan and rhizomes may remain alive below the soil even after treatment."*

Alongside the fourth edition of the TA6 form, the Law Society published updated explanatory notes in 2020. These can be found on the Law Society website at:

> https://www.lawsociety.org.uk/topics/property/transaction-forms

There is no decided authority on the status of the explanatory notes in the context of knotweed but my own view is that they add little. They simply reinforce the obvious distinction between a seller answering "No" and "Not known". They then go on to explain herbicide treatment and excavation.

As well as question 7.8, the questions at 2.1 and 2.2 of the TA6 form may also be relevant.

These read:

> ***"2. Disputes and complaints***
>
> *2.1 Have there been any disputes or complaints regarding this property or a property nearby? If Yes, please give details:*
>
> *2.2 Is the seller aware of anything which might lead to a dispute about the property or a property nearby? If Yes, please give details:"*

The seller can either tick "Yes" or "No" to these.

One can see how these questions might be relevant. For example, a seller knows that there is Japanese knotweed growing in the garden next door. They don't know whether it has actually spread onto their land and so they correctly answer "Not known" at question 7.8 of the TA6 form. They do, however, appreciate that knotweed is an invasive plant which is likely to spread at some point in the future. If they were to tick "No" to question 2.2, they may well fall foul of the word "might" in that question.

CHAPTER TWELVE

LIABILITY

In most cases the representation will come from the Law Society's property information form ("the TA6 form"). I discuss this form in chapter 11.

Ordinarily, the best and most straightforward claim for any buyer is a claim under section 2(1) of the Misrepresentation Act 1967 ("the 1967 Act").

This provides:

> *"Where a person has entered into a contract after a misrepresentation has been made to him by another party thereto and as a result thereof he has suffered loss, then, if the person making the misrepresentation would be liable to damages in respect thereof had the misrepresentation been made fraudulently, that person shall be so liable notwithstanding that the misrepresentation was not made fraudulently, unless he proves that he had reasonable ground to believe and did believe up to the time the contract was made the facts represented were true."*

The first stage is to establish a misrepresentation.

In this respect, there are two kinds of cases, depending on whether the seller ticked "No" or "Not known" at question 7.8 of the TA6 form.

If the seller ticked "No", a claimant need only show that the property was affected by Japanese knotweed in order to show that this representation was untrue. At this stage, the seller's knowledge is irrelevant. Under section 2(1), the burden then shifts to the seller to prove that he did believe it to be true and that he had reasonable grounds to believe it.

The reasonable grounds point is crucial because it renders the question of whether the seller did actually believe it large irrelevant. Instead, in a "No" case, the crucial issue is what steps the seller took to satisfy themselves of the answer.

If the seller ticked "Not known", the buyer needs to show that the seller did know about the knotweed for there to be a misrepresentation in the first place. Of course, if this is proved, the seller could never prove that he believed it and had reasonable grounds to believe it. Therefore, in a "Not known" case, the question of the seller's knowledge becomes crucial.

For both types of claims, a claimant must show that the property was affected by knotweed. Generally, this can be shown in two ways. The first is through direct contemporaneous evidence such as surveyor's photographs, photographs from the estate agent's listing or evidence from a gardener at the property or a neighbour.

The second is through expert evidence. A knotweed expert will often be able to say that knotweed is more likely than not at least X years old. If this is before the sale of the property, the buyer can show that the property was affected.

The relevant time for when the property was affected is not the TA6 itself but the time of sale. This is clear from the wording of section 2(1) which provides for the time period "up to the time the contract was made" and is reinforced by the Law Society's explanatory notes which tell sellers that if they discover new information after completing the TA6 form, they must tell their solicitors of this.

Sometimes, buyers discover knotweed almost immediately after moving in. This is common if they purchase a property in early Spring and the seller had removed dead knotweed canes from the winter. As the growing season starts, knotweed might immediately grow in the garden and become obvious.

In other cases, the delay may be much longer. For instance, in an overgrown garden, buyers might only discover the knotweed growing amongst other undergrowth, perhaps behind a shed or other structure, one or two years after purchasing the property.

As one would imagine, the clearer the evidence is, the more straightforward it will be for the buyer to prove.

If knotweed is established as affecting the property at the time of sale then in a "No" case, the misrepresentation is made out. Under section 2(1), the next question is causation of loss which can be assumed for present purposes.

Under section 2(1) the burden then shifts to the seller to prove that:

i. He believed the representation to be true;

ii. He had reasonable grounds to believe it to be true.

The seller must prove that he believed his answer of "No" to be true. In some cases of obvious concealment (such as the seller cutting back the knotweed shortly before selling the property but leaving the remainder of the garden untouched) this may be difficult for the seller to prove. In other cases, it may be a minor issue because the buyer will be more concerned about the reasonable grounds argument.

The burden on the seller to establish reasonable grounds for his belief is a high one. The leading case on this point remains the Court of Appeal's decision in *Howard Marine & Dredging Co Ltd v Ogden & Sons (Excavations) Ltd* [1978] QB 574.

At 596 Lord Bridge described the effect of the Act in the following terms:

> *"In the course of negotiations leading to a contract the statute imposes an absolute obligation not to state facts which the representor cannot prove he had reasonable ground to believe."*

There is no authority on exactly what a seller must do to satisfy himself that he has reasonable grounds to believe there is no knotweed but my own view is that where a seller has done nothing, and ticks "No" simply because they do not think there is knotweed, that is unlikely to be enough.

If knotweed is established at the property at the time of sale in a "Not known" case, a claimant does need to show that the seller knew there was knotweed. If the seller did not know that there was knotweed, their answer of "Not known" was true and so there was no misrepresentation. The remainder of the claim would not get off the ground in those circumstances.

In my experience of "Not known" cases, the strong claims have been ones where there was a large growth of knotweed and the claimant is able to produce some evidence to show that the seller knew it was knotweed.

The knotweed must have been visible but even a large growth of knotweed alone may not be sufficient if the seller truly did not realise what it was.

Sometimes there may be evidence from a neighbour who will say that he discussed the problem of knotweed with the seller. There may be evidence from a gardener who worked for the seller and told them about the knotweed. There might be circumstantial evidence such as the seller concealing the knotweed.

If a misrepresentation is made out in a "Not known" case, that will generally be the end of the matter. Assuming causation of loss for present purposes, the seller cannot rely on a defence under section 2(1) if it has already been found by the court that they did know about knotweed at the property.

There is also the issue of questions 2.1 and 2.2 on the TA6 form relating to neighbour disputes. I also discuss these in chapter 12. Some of the same evidence as in a "Not known" case under question 7.8 may apply – for instance if there is correspondence with a neighbour discussing the spread of knotweed.

CHAPTER THIRTEEN

RELIANCE

In any misrepresentation claim, the misrepresentation must have been relied on by the representee for there to be a claim.

The burden is on a claimant to prove that the misrepresentation was material, meaning that it was likely to induce them to enter into the contract. Given the prominence of the TA6 and the guidance notes, the questions therein are always likely to be treated as material.

Once the court finds that a misrepresentation was material, there is a presumption that the claimant was induced by it. It was said in *Hayward v Zurich Insurance Co Plc* [2016] UKSC 48 at para 37 that in a case of fraud, "it is very difficult to rebut the presumption". This will include a claim under section 2(1) of the Misrepresentation Act 1967 because of the fiction of fraud.

A claimant does not need to show that the misrepresentation was the sole inducement: it need only have been one of many.

Sometimes, a buyer will not obtain a homebuyer's report but instead will simply rely on the mortgage valuation report. Defendants will often say that they should not be liable for their answers on the TA6 form because the claimant should have had a survey and relied on that instead. There is no direct authority on this in a Japanese knotweed claim but the authorities tend to suggest that this is a weak argument.

In cases of rescission, it is no defence to say that the buyer might have discovered the falsity of the representation by taking reasonable care: *Redgrave v Hurd* (1881) 20 Ch D 1. That rule was paraphrased in *Laurence v Lexcourt Holdings Ltd* [1978] 1 WLR 1128 as follows:

> *"…it is well established that it is no defence to the person who has made the misrepresentation to say 'Oh well, the party who was misled could have checked and found out the facts for himself, and he really has only himself to blame that he relied on me and did not make the inquiries that he might have made.'"*

In a claim for damages under section 2(1) of the 1967 Act, the Court of Appeal accepted, albeit obiter, in *Taberna Europe CDO II Plc v Selskabet AF 1.September 2008 in Bankruptcy* [2016] EWCA Civ 1262, that a defence of contributory negligence may be available in principle.

The caveat to this is that it would likely be an exceptional case where the court did find that it would be just and equitable to make a finding of contributory negligence. The Court of Appeal referred to the judge's references at first instance to "the powerful statements of judicial opinion" in *Redgrave* and other cases. Those statements are summarised in the extract from *Laurence* above.

In the context of a Japanese knotweed claim, those statements are also consistent with the policy underlining the House of Lords' decision in *Smith v Eric S Bush & Harris v Wyre Forest District Council* [1989] 2 WLR 790 regarding a duty of care owed by surveyors to purchasers when carrying out a mortgage valuation survey. I discuss this in chapter 16.

It was held that a surveyor owes a duty to the purchaser despite the contract being between surveyor and mortgage lender because it is reasonably foreseeable that the purchaser will rely on the survey. This applies save for "very expensive houses".

Given this, the court is unlikely to find that a buyer was contributorily negligent for failing to obtain a homebuyer's report or specialist report on Japanese knotweed.

CHAPTER FOURTEEN

RELIANCE

The heads of loss in a misrepresentation claim are the same as in nuisance claims.

Generally, there may be damages for diminution in value, treatment costs and general damages for distress and inconvenience.

For diminution in value, the basic principles are the same in misrepresentation claims as in other claims. Just like diminution in nuisance claims in chapter 6, the court is likely to award residual diminution in value plus treatment costs.

The key difference in misrepresentation claims is that it is the diminution at the time of the sale of the property.

If there are multiple defendants to a single claim, the surveyor will need to be asked to consider diminution at the time of sale for the misrepresentation claim and the current diminution for any other claims.

Those figures may be the same or may be different, usually depending on whether any work has been done to the property since it was purchased.

For treatment costs, the principles are the same as in nuisance claims.

As for distress and inconvenience, again this is likely to run in the same fashion as a nuisance claim. There is no authority on the level of damages but I have had misrepresentation claims where the parties have agreed that the court can take the same approach as the Recorder at trial in *Network Rail v Williams* [2018] EWCA Civ 1514. There, he awarded £350 per year though the knotweed infestation was serious.

CHAPTER FIFTEEN

RESCISSION

Rescission may be difficult where the seller has purchased another property and there is now a chain of transactions to untangle. There is no reason in principle, however, why a buyer cannot rescind a contract on the basis of a misrepresentation about Japanese knotweed.

The principles will be the same as in any other misrepresentation claim.

Firstly, the buyer must not have affirmed the contract. There is no authority on this in a knotweed claim but an example of where the court may find that a buyer had affirmed would be a buyer who had building work done to the property after he had discovered it was affected by Japanese knotweed.

Secondly, there must not have been an undue lapse of time.

In both of these cases, the authorities are clear that there cannot be affirmation or a binding lapse of time until the representee discovered the misrepresentation. In the case of knotweed, there might be some delay before a buyer discovers that there is knotweed at the property and there was at the time of sale.

The court has a discretion to award damages in lieu of rescission under section 2(2) of the Misrepresentation Act 1967. This only applies where the requirements for rescission are met.

If the contract is rescinded, the court may order the seller to indemnify the buyer for obligations to third parties arising from the contract. There is no authority on this in a knotweed claim but this would be likely to include stamp duty charges, surveyor's fees and moving costs.

PART FOUR

PROFESSIONAL NEGLIGENCE CLAIMS AGAINST SURVEYORS

CHAPTER SIXTEEN

DUTY OF CARE

There are three types of pre-purchase survey: a mortgage valuation report, a homebuyer's report and a building survey.

A mortgage valuation report is done for the benefit of the mortgage lender but it is well-established that a surveyor who carries out such a report owes a duty of care to the purchaser because it is reasonably foreseeable that the purchaser will rely on it: *Smith v Eric S Bush & Harris v Wyre Forest District Council* [1989] 2 WLR 790 (HL).

In principle, a surveyor will therefore always owe a duty of care in negligence to a purchaser of a residential property. The exceptions may be commercial premises or what was described in *Smith & Harris* as "very expensive houses". There is no guidance in respect of this but given that the average house price in the UK at the time of writing is £256,000, I would suggest that it is difficult to see how anything less than 3 times this value could be described as "very expensive".

For homebuyer's reports and building surveys, the surveyor will also have a contract with the purchasers directly.

The duty of care will normally be the same in contract or negligence: to act to the standards expected of a reasonably competent surveyor.

I have never known it to be argued that a surveyor should not be expected to identify and report on Japanese knotweed if it is present.

Where the duty of care may differ in respect of the three different kinds of survey is the extent of the inspection required. For instance, a mortgage valuation report may not require a surveyor to look at neighbouring properties whereas for a homebuyer's report, readily visible knotweed on neighbouring land right up against the boundary with the subject property may be something which the surveyor is expected to identify and report.

CHAPTER SEVENTEEN

BREACH OF DUTY

The nature of establish breach against a surveyor will depend on the time of year of their inspection. The growing season for Japanese knotweed is normally from around March to October. Outside of the growing season, Japanese knotweed stems will die back and leave dead winter canes which remain unless removed.

Depending on the date of the survey, the question will be whether the surveyor should have identified live knotweed growth or dead winter canes.

The starting point for a claimant is to show that knotweed was visible at the date of inspection. It is not enough to say that there was knotweed at the property because this could have been concealed by the seller cutting it back or covering it. Alternatively, the knotweed might have been behind a shed or hidden in thick undergrowth where it was not there to be seen.

Knotweed may be visible in photographs taken by the surveyor on the day. Often there may be additional photographs taken by the surveyor which were not included in the report itself. A claimant will normally ask for these when sending a letter of claim.

There may also be photographs showing knotweed from the estate agent's listing which can normally be checked by searching online.

If Japanese knotweed is present in a prominent position in the garden but photographs show that it was not present on inspection, this may tend to suggest that the seller cut it back or concealed it. If the seller carried out a comprehensive makeover of the garden, this may not be surprising. If only the knotweed was removed, this may suggest that the seller deliberately concealed it.

This may make a claim weaker against a surveyor but stronger against a seller or vice versa.

If Japanese knotweed was present at the property but was obscured behind a shed or was located in undergrowth, it may be that a reasonable surveyor would not be expected to have identified it. Where there is a shed or some other obstacle, this will often turn on whether the knotweed was growing high enough to be visible above it. This will only apply to surveys carried out during the growing season.

As discussed in chapter 16, the type of survey may affect the scope of the inspection required. If there is Japanese knotweed growing in a neighbouring garden, right up against the boundary with the subject property, again the question will be whether this was visible. It may have been visible when looking out of an upstairs window or it may be that it was visible from the garden the fence. In some cases, there will be a palisade fence where knotweed can clearly be seen through the gaps rather than a solid fence.

All of these points will need evidence from an expert surveyor to comment on breach of duty.

CHAPTER EIGHTEEN

CAUSATION AND DAMAGES

A claimant must show that had the surveyor commented on Japanese knotweed, they would either have refused to purchase the property or would have only purchased it for a lower price.

Defendants may suspect such evidence to be self-serving but it is normally very difficult to challenge.

Where there is one or more concurrent claims in nuisance against a neighbouring landowner or against the seller for misrepresentation, each will generally be severally liable. I anticipate that they would not be jointly and severally liable because there is a different cause of action against each. The court might apportion damages between defendants itself or may award the claimant damages in full against each and leave it to the defendants to argue apportionment in a part 20 claim.

For damages in professional negligence, the starting point is the same as a nuisance claim, namely the residual diminution in value of the property plus treatment costs.

The timing of the diminution will be when the loss arises: *Philips v Ward* [1956] 1 WLR 471. In a knotweed case, this will normally be the time of sale.

An expert surveyor who is reporting on diminution in value will therefore need to be asked to comment on the diminution in value at the time of sale rather than the present diminution as in a nuisance claim. If there are concurrent claims both in nuisance and professional negligence, the surveyor will need to report on both.

For treatment costs, it does not matter when the knotweed encroached provided it was present and should have been reported on at the time of the survey.

A claimant may also be able to recover general damages for distress and inconvenience as in a nuisance claim. I discuss this in chapter 8.

As for the cost of any repairs, this would normally be a freestanding issue based on whether or not the surveyor negligently failed to report on the presence of any defects or damage to the property.

PART FIVE

PROFESSIONAL NEGLIGENCE CLAIMS AGAINST CONVEYANCERS

CHAPTER NINETEEN

CLAIMS AGAINST CONVEYANCERS

Most professional negligence claims will be against surveyors but there are cases where a claimant may consider a claim against a conveyancer.

The starting point is that a buyer's conveyancer will owe them a duty both in contract and in tort.

In contract, there may be an express term in the retainer or alternatively there will be the duty to act with reasonable care and skill implied into the contract by section 13 of the Supply of Goods and Services Act 1982.

In practical terms, the standard of care will not differ between contract and negligence.

In a standard purchase of a residential property, it would normally be expected of a conveyancer to ensure that the seller provided a completed copy of the Law Society's property information form ("the TA6 form"). If they did not, the buyer would not be able to rely on the various answers given within that form, including about Japanese knotweed at question 7.8.

If a conveyancer did not request this and it was not provided, the buyer may well have a claim. Likewise, a seller who did provide a form which answered "Yes" to question 7.8 but which was not then communicated to the buyer. In those circumstances, the buyer may well have a claim.

Sometimes, sellers will ask not to use the Law Society's standard conditions of sale, usually meaning also not using the TA6 form. This can be common with sales by local authorities, who often use their own standard terms of sale.

Depending on those terms, the seller may well not have to make any representation about Japanese knotweed at all. Alternatively, the terms may well exclude liability for any representations. A buyer may choose to accept these terms but the increased risks to the buyer would need to be explained in order for them to make an informed decision about this. If not, there may well be a breach of duty by their conveyancer.

In purchases of commercial properties, differing terms of this kind will often be common.

In terms of damages, these will generally be the same as in claims against surveyors.

PART SIX

PROCEDURE

CHAPTER TWENTY

LIMITATION

Nuisance claims are based on tort so the relevant limitation period is six years from the accrual of the cause of action under section 2 of the Limitation Act 1980 or 3 years from date of knowledge under section 14A of the Act. There is then a longstop date of 15 years under section 14B of the Act.

In nuisance claims, there is not yet any decided authority on limitation. I am involved in a number of cases where limitation is in issue and no doubt there will be some binding authority on this in the future.

Following the Court of Appeal's reasoning in *Network Rail v Williams* [2018] EWCA Civ 1514 that the presence of Japanese knotweed rhizomes in the soil amounts to a nuisance because it is an interference with the amenity value of a property, the loss accrues on encroachment. That is uncontroversial.

Where encroachment occurred before the defendant was under a duty to treat, the loss alone would not amount to the accrual of a cause of action. There must be duty and breach as well as loss for there to be a cause of action so in that case, it seems that the cause of action could only accrue once the defendant came under a duty and was in breach of that duty. For historic encroachment, this will generally mean a duty and breach from 2012/13 given the general approach on constructive knowledge which I discuss in chapter 3.

Where there has been encroachment, duty and breach for more than six years, claimants will rely on the principle of a continuing nuisance. That is to say, the clock continues to run so long as the defendant is in breach.

If knotweed encroached in 2013 but a defendant only started to properly treat in 2018, the claimant would argue that the six years runs from 2018.

I have experience of two particular arguments from defendants. Both of these have arisen in cases where I am acting for the claimants so I may be unfairly paraphrasing them.

The first is to say that any further growth on a claimant's property is growth emanating from the knotweed that originally encroached. Therefore, the further growth does not reset the clock and the six years runs from the first breach.

My view is that this is a very fact-specific argument and would require a finding from that court that a single rhizome of knotweed encroached under the boundary and then all knotweed on the claimant's side since that date has emanated from that single rhizome. I have not seen a case where any expert has been able to give such precise evidence and my own view is that this is unrealistic.

The second argument is that under the principle of a continuing nuisance, a claimant can only recover the losses from within the last six years. That is common in tree root cases where particular cracking can be attributed to subsidence from different years. In a knotweed case, however, there is generally a single loss, namely the residual diminution in value after treatment. In those circumstances, a defendant may argue that this whole loss is out of time and should be disallowed.

I expect that the court would reject this argument given that when considering a single loss, to disallow that whole loss because it originated before the six year limitation period would be to undermine the principle of a continuing nuisance and effectively to set a hard limit of six years. The compromise position of having the six year limit but being able to ascertain which damages arose before and after, as in a tree root case, is simply not possible in a knotweed case.

What the court decides remains to be seen.

As for date of knowledge under section 14B of the Limitation Act 1980, the section includes the word “negligence” but it will apply to nuisance claims. As has been made clear in the authorities relating to tree root claims, there is no real difference between nuisance and negligence in most contexts.

Date of knowledge may well be academic in many cases if the court accepts that the clock continues to run while a defendant remains in breach. Imagine a case where knotweed encroached in 2010, the defendant came under a duty to treat in 2012, the claimant discovered knotweed at their property emanating from the defendant’s land in 2015 and the defendant started treating in 2017. In that case, the 3 year period from date of knowledge would expire in 2018 but the six year period from end of breach would expire in 2023. In that situation, the period from date of knowledge adds nothing. Date of knowledge may become more important if the court did find that that a claim for residual diminution in value and treatment costs was disallowable if it originated more than six years earlier.

As to knowledge, it is knowledge of “the material facts about the damage” per section 14A(six)(a) of the Act which in a knotweed claim will mean knowledge that Japanese knotweed is present at a claimant’s property. It may arguably also mean that this will cause a diminution in value of the property. There is no authority about that.

Also, it is knowledge of the three factors in section 14(A)(8) of the Act namely attributability, the identity of the defendant and if relevant, the identity of a third party. In this context, attributability is likely to mean knowledge that the knotweed has originated from the defendant’s land.

In misrepresentation claims, the limitation period for a claim for damages under section 2(1) of the Misrepresentation Act 19six7 is six years under sections 2 and or/ 9 of Limitation Act 1980.

On the authority of *Green v Eadie* [2012] Ch 363, the limitation period runs from exchange of contracts rather than the misrepresentation or completion. In that case, it was held that the loss arose when the buyer became committed to the purchase. That occurred on exchange. At that point, the cause of action accrued: see para 57.

In a fraudulent misrepresentation claim or where there is deliberate concealment, a claimant may rely on section 32 of the Limitation Act 1980 which provides that the limitation period does not start to run until the claimant has discovered the fraud or concealment.

In professional negligence claims, a surveyor may have had a contract with the claimant. Certainly, in a claim against a conveyancer, there will be a contract. Where a surveyor conducted a mortgage valuation, they will owe a duty of care to a purchaser in negligence but there is no contractual relationship.

Therefore, depending on the circumstances, the relevant limitation period may be in contract, negligence or both. It is well-established that a duty in contract can run concurrently with a duty of care in negligence: *Henderson v Merrett Syndicates* [1995] 2 AC 145.

The primary limitation period for both is six years but for limitation will often be more favourable to claimants in negligence than in contract. For example, there is the 3 year period post-date of knowledge under section 14B of the Limitation Act 1980 for negligence claims.

It will normally be easier to identify when the cause of action accrued in a professional negligence claim because the negligence will relate to a specific act (e.g. the survey) rather than a continuing nuisance over a long period of time.

CHAPTER TWENTY-ONE

COSTS AND ALLOCATION

For many Japanese knotweed claims, damages will be comfortably above the £10,000 threshold for small claims. The usual costs rules will apply and depending on the value, the amount of evidence and the complexity of the issues, the case will either be allocated to the fast track or multi-track.

In cases where the value of the property is lower, damages may not reach the £10,000 threshold. If a claim is issued, the court may well allocate it to the small claims track in which case the very limited provision for costs would apply. In most knotweed cases, this will make it uneconomic for a claimant to fund the cost of litigation.

It may be that even in a low value claim, the amount and complexity of evidence would lead the court to allocate it to the fast track or multi-track. Of course, from a claimant's perspective, they will not know this until directions stage, so they would have to take the risk in paying the issue fee and litigating the early stages of the claim before finding out.

What about a borderline case, where a claimant might seek damages of £15,000 but the court ultimately awards £8,000? The defendant will likely argue that the claimant unreasonably overvalued their claim and should be limited to small claims costs.

The court has a wide discretion on costs in these circumstances and so different judges will inevitably take different approaches. Many judges will say that if a claim has been allocated to the fast track or multi-track, the normal costs rules apply, even if the ultimate value awarded is below the small claims threshold.

My own view based on experience of claims in general is that if the claim could reasonably be valued at more than £10,000, the court will be likely to award costs even if the damages awarded are ultimately less. Only in a case where it was or should have been obvious that damages could not be above £10,000 will the court refuse to award normal costs.

Assuming a claim has not been allocated to the small claims track, in which case part 36 no longer applies, the parties can make part 36 offers which will provide for

reasonable costs in the normal way, even if the sums agreed are below £10,000. It may well be that a claim would be worth more than £10,000 if successful in trial but the claimant accepts a discount to account for litigation risk. That does not then put the case into the position of a small claim.

PART SEVEN

OTHER INVASIVE SPECIES

CHAPTER TWENTY-TWO

OTHER INVASIVE SPECIES

Japanese knotweed is the most widely known invasive species of plant in the UK but there are many others.

As well as Japanese knotweed, formerly known as *Fallopica japonica* and now known as *Reynoutria japonica*, there is a similar species, *Reynoutria sachalinensis* aka "giant knotweed" which is also invasive.

There is also a variety of Japanese knotweed known as "dwarf Japanese knotweed" (*Reynoutria japnonica var. 'Compacta'*) which, as the name suggests, is smaller in size.

In the context of misrepresentation claims, the TA6 form refers to "Japanese knotweed". There is no authority on whether this extends to the dwarf variety and how the variety would affect the various questions in a claim under section 2(1) of the Misrepresentation Act 1967. There are arguments either way and no doubt this will be an important case in the future.

Apart from knotweed, a common invasive plant in the UK is giant hogweed *(Heracleum mantegazzianum)*. Unlike Japanese knotweed, giant hogweed is toxic to humans. This gives rise to new potential claims: for example, a landowner who fails to control a growth of giant hogweed which then injures walkers using a public footpath.

Himalayan balsam *(Impatiens glandulifera)* is another invasive plant. Unlike giant hogweed, it is not toxic.

Both are "controlled waste" within the meaning of the Environmental Protection Act 1990 and so must be disposed of in a designated fashion in the same way as Japanese knotweed.

This inevitably makes it more difficult for a landowner to develop their land which was part of the ratio in *Network Rail v Williams* [2018] EWCA Civ 1514 as to why the presence of Japanese knotweed could amount to a nuisance.

As to diminution in value, neither would seem to be caught by question 7.8 of the TA6 form though if the seller knows of them and that they might spread, their presence might be caught by questions 2.1 and 2.2 of the TA6: see chapter 11.

There is an argument as to whether a surveyor will be expected to identify them and report on them in a survey.

For farmers, another problematic species is black-grass *(Alopecurus myosuroides)*. This grass has developed herbicide-resistance and competes with crops for nutrients in the soil. The problem is well-known to farmers and one can see the building blocks for a nuisance claim.

MORE BOOKS BY LAW BRIEF PUBLISHING

'Covid-19, Homeworking and the Law – The Essential Guide to Employment and GDPR Issues' by Forbes Solicitors
'Covid-19, Force Majeure and Frustration of Contracts – The Essential Guide' by Keith Markham
'Covid-19 and Criminal Law – The Essential Guide' by Ramya Nagesh
'Covid-19 and Family Law in England and Wales – The Essential Guide' by Safda Mahmood
'A Practical Guide to the Law of Unlawful Eviction and Harassment – 2nd Edition' by Stephanie Lovegrove
'Covid-19, Residential Property, Equity Release and Enfranchisement – The Essential Guide' by Paul Sams and Louise Uphill
'Covid-19, Brexit and the Law of Commercial Leases – The Essential Guide' by Mark Shelton
'A Practical Guide to Costs in Personal Injury Claims – 2nd Edition' by Matthew Hoe
'A Practical Guide to the General Data Protection Regulation (GDPR) – 2nd Edition' by Keith Markham
'Ellis on Credit Hire – Sixth Edition' by Aidan Ellis & Tim Kevan
'A Practical Guide to Working with Litigants in Person and McKenzie Friends in Family Cases' by Stuart Barlow
'Protecting Unregistered Brands: A Practical Guide to the Law of Passing Off' by Lorna Brazell
'A Practical Guide to Secondary Liability and Joint Enterprise Post-Jogee' by Joanne Cecil & James Mehigan
'A Practical Guide to the Pre-Action RTA Claims Protocol for Personal Injury Lawyers' by Antonia Ford
'A Practical Guide to Neighbour Disputes and the Law' by Alexander Walsh
'A Practical Guide to Forfeiture of Leases' by Mark Shelton
'A Practical Guide to Coercive Control for Legal Practitioners and Victims' by Rachel Horman

'A Practical Guide to Rights Over Airspace and Subsoil' by Daniel Gatty
'Tackling Disclosure in the Criminal Courts – A Practitioner's Guide' by Narita Bahra QC & Don Ramble
'A Practical Guide to the Law of Driverless Cars – Second Edition' by Alex Glassbrook, Emma Northey & Scarlett Milligan
'A Practical Guide to TOLATA Claims' by Greg Williams
'Artificial Intelligence – The Practical Legal Issues' by John Buyers
'A Practical Guide to the Law of Prescription in Scotland' by Andrew Foyle
'A Practical Guide to the Construction and Rectification of Wills and Trust Instruments' by Edward Hewitt
'A Practical Guide to the Law of Bullying and Harassment in the Workplace' by Philip Hyland
'How to Be a Freelance Solicitor: A Practical Guide to the SRA-Regulated Freelance Solicitor Model' by Paul Bennett
'A Practical Guide to Prison Injury Claims' by Malcolm Johnson
'A Practical Guide to the Small Claims Track' by Dominic Bright
'A Practical Guide to Advising Clients at the Police Station' by Colin Stephen McKeown-Beaumont
'A Practical Guide to Antisocial Behaviour Injunctions' by Iain Wightwick
'Practical Mediation: A Guide for Mediators, Advocates, Advisers, Lawyers, and Students in Civil, Commercial, Business, Property, Workplace, and Employment Cases' by Jonathan Dingle with John Sephton
'The Mini-Pupillage Workbook' by David Boyle
'A Practical Guide to Crofting Law' by Brian Inkster
'A Practical Guide to Spousal Maintenance' by Liz Cowell
'A Practical Guide to the Law of Domain Names and Cybersquatting' by Andrew Clemson
'A Practical Guide to the Law of Gender Pay Gap Reporting' by Harini Iyengar

'A Practical Guide to the Rights of Grandparents in Children Proceedings' by Stuart Barlow
'NHS Whistleblowing and the Law' by Joseph England
'Employment Law and the Gig Economy' by Nigel Mackay & Annie Powell
'A Practical Guide to Noise Induced Hearing Loss (NIHL) Claims' by Andrew Mckie, Ian Skeate, Gareth McAloon
'An Introduction to Beauty Negligence Claims – A Practical Guide for the Personal Injury Practitioner' by Greg Almond
'Intercompany Agreements for Transfer Pricing Compliance' by Paul Sutton
'Zen and the Art of Mediation' by Martin Plowman
'A Practical Guide to the SRA Principles, Individual and Law Firm Codes of Conduct 2019 – What Every Law Firm Needs to Know' by Paul Bennett
'A Practical Guide to Adoption for Family Lawyers' by Graham Pegg
'A Practical Guide to Industrial Disease Claims' by Andrew Mckie & Ian Skeate
'A Practical Guide to Redundancy' by Philip Hyland
'A Practical Guide to Vicarious Liability' by Mariel Irvine
'A Practical Guide to Applications for Landlord's Consent and Variation of Leases' by Mark Shelton
'A Practical Guide to Relief from Sanctions Post-Mitchell and Denton' by Peter Causton
'A Practical Guide to Equity Release for Advisors' by Paul Sams
'A Practical Guide to the Law Relating to Food' by Ian Thomas
'A Practical Guide to Financial Services Claims' by Chris Hegarty
'The Law of Houses in Multiple Occupation: A Practical Guide to HMO Proceedings' by Julian Hunt
'A Practical Guide to Unlawful Eviction and Harassment' by Stephanie Lovegrove
'Occupiers, Highways and Defective Premises Claims: A Practical Guide Post-Jackson – 2nd Edition' by Andrew Mckie

'A Practical Guide to Financial Ombudsman Service Claims' by Adam Temple & Robert Scrivenor
'A Practical Guide to Advising Schools on Employment Law' by Jonathan Holden
'A Practical Guide to Running Housing Disrepair and Cavity Wall Claims: 2nd Edition' by Andrew Mckie & Ian Skeate
'A Practical Guide to Holiday Sickness Claims – 2nd Edition' by Andrew Mckie & Ian Skeate
'Arguments and Tactics for Personal Injury and Clinical Negligence Claims' by Dorian Williams
'A Practical Guide to Drone Law' by Rufus Ballaster, Andrew Firman, Eleanor Clot
'A Practical Guide to Compliance for Personal Injury Firms Working With Claims Management Companies' by Paul Bennett
'A Practical Guide to Dog Law for Owners and Others' by Andrea Pitt
'RTA Allegations of Fraud in a Post-Jackson Era: The Handbook – 2nd Edition' by Andrew Mckie
'RTA Personal Injury Claims: A Practical Guide Post-Jackson' by Andrew Mckie
'On Experts: CPR35 for Lawyers and Experts' by David Boyle
'An Introduction to Personal Injury Law' by David Boyle
'A Practical Guide to Subtle Brain Injury Claims' by Pankaj Madan

These books and more are available to order online direct from the publisher at www.lawbriefpublishing.com, where you can also read free sample chapters. For any queries, contact us on 0844 587 2383 or mail@lawbriefpublishing.com.

Our books are also usually in stock at www.amazon.co.uk with free next day delivery for Prime members, and at good legal bookshops such as Wildy & Sons.

We are regularly launching new books in our series of practical day-to-day practitioners' guides. Visit our website and join our free newsletter to be kept informed and to receive special offers, free chapters, etc.

You can also follow us on Twitter at www.twitter.com/lawbriefpub.

www.ingramcontent.com/pod-product-compliance
Ingram Content Group UK Ltd.
Pitfield, Milton Keynes, MK11 3LW, UK
UKHW020150290926
15471UKWH00004B/788

9 781913 715557